Monster Fashion

Monster Fashion

Jarret Keene

Manic D Press
San Francisco

Thanks to the following individuals, for their friendship and support in the writing of this book: Gaylord Brewer, Van K. Brock, Jim Daniels, John Fenstermaker, Douglas Fowler, Barbara Hamby, Denis Johnson, Jennifer Joseph, David Kirby, Todd James Pierce, Ernest Rehder, Virgil Suarez, William Trowbridge, Ryan G. Van Cleave, Miles Garrett Watson, and Wyatt Wyatt. And special thanks to my wife Jennifer, the Keene family, the Prendes family, Bruce and Rosemary Reid, and Paul and Patricia Jacob.

Published with the generous assistance of the California Arts Council. The publisher wishes to thank the estate of Jack Kirby, Ken Steacy, and TwoMorrows Publishing. Printed in Canada.

Cover illustration: Jack Kirby
Illustration ink & color: Ken Steacy
Cover design: Scott Idleman/Blink

Library of Congress Cataloging-in-Publication Data

Keene, Jarret, 1973-
Monster fashion / Jarret Keene.
    p. cm.
ISBN 0-916397-77-7 (trade pbk. original : alk. paper)
1. Popular culture--Poetry. I. Title.
PS3611.E34 M66 2002
811'.6--dc21
                    2001008629

Contents

"Stop, drop, and roll won't help you in Hell."
— church sign on Highway 421
near Sunshine, Kentucky

ONE

After Watching a Local High School Stage Production of George Romero's "Night of the Living Dead"

Dressed in decaying suits and ties, wrinkled zombies
threaten the shiny-faced and hiply-attired.
The kids are all right, the living ones anyway.

They've locked themselves in a room.
With grunge rock and a plastic axe,
they repulse the flesh-eaters clawing at the door.

Momentarily, the music seems to help,
until the monsters start mashing to the beat,
mocking it, turning the teens' noise against them.

It's ugly to watch, this corruption, this soiling
of what was once fresh, if a little petulant.
For all the good it did, kids might've blasted Welk.

Sure, the stage creaks, lines are mangled, and the effects
are less special than in the original no-budget 1968 classic.
But the ending haunts me: Upon being partially devoured,

the young rise up, features dulled, arms extended,
jerking like the other rancid puppets,
in love with death as only the young can be.

Haunted

The moon is a carcass.
Crickets scream their bodies raw. Then laughter.

Who are all these fools at your door?
Why do they now speak truth?
Tricked or mistreated, someone asks.
To which you reply, Were the bodies buried or eaten?

To repeat this message, write your name
In blood.

Your bag is filled with zombie flesh.
Worse, someone bothered to candy the razorblades.
These needles are for your eyes.
Yet even now pumpkins carve your face.

Better dig a grave.

Monsters limp into your apartment.
Ghouls shriek at the mirrors.
On the sofa, poltergeists play solitaire.
In the kitchen, vampires call your mother long-distance.
Skeletons shove pizzas into their ribcages, pour cola
Over gnashing teeth.
The werewolves shave each other.
Mummies unwind themselves to wipe Frankenstein's ass.

Make popcorn. Pray everyone
Leaves.

Monster Fashion

I. Vampire Dress

Sleek and fluid.

Cross-backed
And black as a blood clot.
Gently falls to below a porcelain
Calf. Side-slitted,

This satin of insomniacs,
This silk of Satan,
Of the nether saint, is
Enzyme-washed and
Softer than a bat's belly.
Under the dark, slim shape,

A wired top for an empress's fit.
Accessorize with chain belt,
City sunglasses, suede sling bag,
Leather stilettos, upside down
Crucifix.

Never wash. Always wear.

II. Frankenstein Jeans

Stonewashed, sandblasted
And plenty tough.
Our sturdiest denim is
More than enough.
Roomier yet through the seat,
Thigh. Broken-in, zip

Fly. Off-seamed for a
Gargantuan fit. Green bar
Tacking, solid rivets.

Cargo front; back
Pockets welt. Don't forget
The polypropylene belt.

Heavyweight thick-gauge stitch.
Sits a bit lower on
A reanimate's hips.
Bolted, cuffed, doughnut
Shanked. This frayed pair
Can stop a tank.

III. Wolfman Cardigan

Long, luxuriant lambswool hides
Hairy hides. Sheep's clothing

Never felt so perfectly stealthy.
Wash, rinse, comb, blow-dry,

Tease. No snags in this drag.
You're sure to steal serious

Veal in our venal garment.
It's certain you'll ascertain more

Mutton in our imported were-
Wear. Buy now, because these days

Everybody's endangered and there's always
Someone panting in your ear. Look soft.

IV. Ghost Sandals

Crepe leather soles creep
Across a crow's shadow. Antiqued
Silver finish buckle. Waxed
Calfskin heel. These must be twilight's
Footwear. Let's try them on.

Now skulk sensibly in comfort,
With style. Whole sizes only:
Brown, dark brown, black, ground
Zero (at center), anti-matter (below),
Plus chaos, and (finally but not shown)
Infinity. Hardly heavier than a child
Bride's veil. Mary, God of Mothers,
Tramped to Golgotha on a pair
Of open toe slingbacks. Got there

Just in time.

Inside Mystery Funhouse

What's scary is that these mirrors
Distort nothing. What's scary is that this place
Resembles your house. Sulfur-stinking clowns
Tickle your children. Scar-faced carnies

Caress your wife before strapping her down
To a chair that looks like the one in your den.
Sideshow screamers talk back to your mother.
The tunnel of love is a CAT-scan.

The cotton candy is on fire. See the human lobster
Shooting up with drugs made in your sink.
See God in the palm of a transsexual's hand.
Witness the power of the teen vomit machine.

What is the mystery of the Mystery Funhouse?
Its address is a secret kept by snake charmers.
Its locks are impossible to pick from the inside.
There are no signs with red arrows indicating

The closest way out.

In Honor of the Inauguration of the World's First Baby Abandonment Station

Once, wading drunkenly through a street-lit dumpster,
I rescued a bicycle tire, rolled it back to my dorm room
where I hammered-and-nailed it to the wall
in such a way that allowed it to spin.
The next morning, hungover and bored,
I decided to make it a work of found art.
I splattered it with acrylic paint, burned it
with a borrowed acetylene torch, glued to it
some stuffed animals and *Hustler* clippings.
I called the piece "Wheel of Confusion,"
after the Black Sabbath song.
Looking back, the title was appropriate,
since the thing succeeded in confusing
my roommate: business major, pragmatist,
patient with but wary of the strange and obscene.
He walked in and said, "What's this?"
"I'm not sure," I said. For a time, we had fun
spinning the wheel whenever one of us bombed
a test or bounced a check or generally failed at life.
But I grew bored again, and after a few beers
went back to the dumpster, wrenched from its rot
what looked like a CPR dummy. I washed him,
dressed him in my clothes, but seeing a faceless
dummy wearing shades and a Nirvana t-shirt was odd.
"He's ugly," my roommate confirmed.
So I stripped the dummy, returned him
to the dumpster's fetid embrace. An hour passed
before waves of guilt washed over me,
but I did not go back, because the dummy wasn't real,
just a hunk of cold, useless rubber.
Years later I write this down, and now, with my head
spinning in pure confusion, let it be known
the name I've given my dummy is Vincent.

RPM

"The FBI investigation determined that 'Louie Louie' was
unintelligible at any speed." — Dave Marsh

Not true. I once played the song
    at the standard 45 rpm and experienced
a wealth of pornography ("I feel
    the rose down in her hair"). Then,
at a slower 33-1/3, a whiff of sulfur,
    crudity bordering on the psychotic
("Aww, it's almost over now").
    The needle seeped its ugly truth
down into the black groove.
    Might just as well have injected
my own veins, it was that scary.
    Wishing to escape the shadows,
I moved toward the sun's crisp rays,
    where speed offers safety, where at 78
rpm "a fine, little girl waits for me."
    I closed my eyes. I could see this girl
skipping through a field of bright flowers,
    laughing. But then I also saw Special
Agent Harvey sitting in a special lab
    capable of translating smutty rock'n'roll
lyrics. Nerves jangled by coffee, he fidgets.
    He does his best to concentrate, to listen
again to the single slowed down, stupefied,
    wondering if the young singer had been
given sedatives and asked to howl through
    the haze despite the weight of his tongue,
his mouth's lack of feeling. "Kid sounds old,"
    the tech jokes. Harvey nods, sips coffee.
All the while the needle scratches with its
    pristine claw. And I'm clawing my own
face, so I can't watch the tech hijack the song
    into another realm, where science always
fails in the face of the mystery of teenagers

and cars and fast food. Either affirm the glory
of nonsense or get the hell out of their way.
    Pay homage to the power of gonadal
excitement or die. Does anyone get to dream
    classic riffs for free? *Deus ex cartoona?*
No, rather, it's the G-men versus the Kingsmen.
    What can match the knuckleheaded
energies of Louiemania? At any speed, God
    is unintelligible. He *is* Speed. Speed is
the Barrier of Sound that is Darkness. Speed
    is the weapon that kills, or at best maims.
Speed does not answer to the Transportation
    of Obscene Material. Speed does not bow
to the moral hygiene of the Bureau-crat.
    Speed is not picked up by most modern
criminological tools and state-of-the-art
    surveillance techniques. Speed has never
heard of Paul Revere and the Raiders,
    though Speed will speak through them
from time to time. Speed is the sound
    of one guitar bashing your skull
in the wilderness. Gram Parsons sang,
    "O Lord, grant me speed," but what
he was really asking for was the divine
    spark of madness. And he got it.
But the FBI didn't want it. They wanted
    greasy fingerprints. They wanted stained
underwear. They wanted a smoking gun.
    What they got was nothing but the jungle
rhythms and the clanging trash cans that
    haunted their dreams. They got the
Monster Whose Name Is Zero. They got
    Squat and the Air Biscuits. The Egg
of Absolute Nada. Supersquare,
    the government could never fathom
the Sublime. Tons of tax dollars, and
    zippo. Meanwhile, there's this pimply-
faced kid in his room going, *Duh duh duh,*
    duh duh, duh duh duh.

What Denis Johnson Said When I Gave Him a Pair of X-Ray Specs

Still nothing. Breasts are just
Breasts. And I already knew about
That one's lack of underwear.
What, did you expect
Me to froth at the mouth
In my attempt to penetrate
Clothes? Too bad.
Look deeper? Flesh and blood
Give way to white bone
Just like a splatter movie.

Hearts? Shit. They beat
As stupidly as before.

Shower
for Janet Leigh

Whenever Hitch yells "cut," Tony makes
Another lame joke, another pornographic
Gesture with the plastic knife. Shanghaied
To a tiny studio-lot bathroom, trapped
In the damp belly of Hitch's angles.
Clammy moleskin sliding from her breasts.
"Corpse-like" contacts burning her eyes.
She glances up toward the showerhead
As countless electricians peer down
From the scaffolding. She sighs, wipes her brow,
Prepares herself for the rolling camera.
How many more baptisms? For the first
Twenty takes, it was all very symbolic:
Her character comes clean, her soul,
And so on. Now it's just routine.
After she slides down the tiled wall,
Collapses over the edge, lands awkwardly—
Face squished against the floor—thirty more
Times, she'll grab a towel, lock herself
In an equally cramped dressing room,
Meditate a moment before driving home.
Then she'll wrap Christmas presents
And listen for carolers. If they don't show,
She'll mix a whiskey sour, spin a record,
Something mellow—no violins.
And she'll sin in her dreams tonight,
Ready for tomorrow's waters.

Ava Gardner, Queen of Earthquakes

I. The Sinatra Years

Ava, this Sinatra fellow means trouble: his voice is gin,
    but his touch is the devil's testicle, his kiss a gold-
plated revolver. Your white pills are no match
    for the heart-stripping force of a black diamond.
Reconsider his deadly ingredients: a nylon guitar string
    quickens the pulse, candlelight singes the brain,
basil inflames the loins, and wine offers salvation
    only after you absolve it of guilt. Who told you
every antidote is a venom in reverse? But the music!
    My God, his hard-boiled romanticism! The man's
haunted passion and stark irony could wound for hours
    without so much as destroy. Even today there are
men who crank transistors and pretend to be *mafioso*.
    Last we spoke, your gut-shot heart had been left
to spoil, a blown tire on a roadside of dead celebrities,
    their bodies twitching under flash-photography
hailstorms. In between bolts, why not collect
    the blackest pistols? Go ahead: Smuggle one
into your purse and do as follows: Place pillow
    over barrel. Squeeze trigger. Catch feathers.
Hear every blasted note touch your skin.
    Let each object in the bedroom resonate
like an angel's vestment. Listen, Ava. Listen to the toaster.
    Hark, the faux-leopard coat. Trace the radiant arc
of his last swaggering crescendo. Put the vinyl
    to your tongue. Taste the single groove that leads
to the needle, the black spider, Satan. Suck, cauterize
    with fire, bandage, immediately amputate.
There are no victims here, only punishment. A vague,
    terminal power over women. The talent to savage
a beast, to sleep with a torch song that softly cremates.

II. Ava's Shade Speaks

My face: gored by a young bull,
treated with therapeutic massage,
steam and vapors. The invisible mark
a deathbed curse. In Mexico, there is only
mutilation, the sick dust of make-up.
And to think I'd survived the glint
of a maid's butcher knife. I remember
Hughes's slap dislocating my jaw,
but I didn't fall. Instead,
I fractured his skull with a brass statuette
of his XF-11 photo-reconnaissance plane.
Crack! I cursed him, his impotence,
his Mormon bodyguards.
That night I cooked Southern fried chicken
and mashed potatoes, and let me tell you,
I'm the best gravy maker on this planet.
He chewed slowly; he was no stranger to blood.
He was no swordsman either, but he could eat.

My gallbladder: surgically removed in Spain.
Frank's Catholic bodyguards brought sprays
of orchids. Hemingway touched the incision
like a priest who fears his own death.
"I kill pleasure for animals," he confided.

My uterus: scraped, burned, removed.
I've apologized to all Romeos, those glib
destroyers of sex, who require a radical
inner ugliness to fuel an otherwise bland
outer greatness. My advice? If someone
brings a gun to a knife fight, break his legs.
Place your hands on your lover's face.
Keep them there or he'll seduce other women.

My heart: a prostitute. I married my first husband
at age twenty. But who will save you from fate's

jury-rigged screenplay? Will anyone confess that
the mattress is bullet-riddled? When you're bored,
you take up bullfighting. Sometimes you trap yourself
as a hunter traps an animal. Sometimes you roll
your car over and walk away. Once,
in a Chicago nightclub, I locked myself in the restroom.
People outside had torn pieces of my black
evening gown for souvenirs. I'd have given them each
a scrap, but my handbag contained a gun,
amphetamines, a matador's phone number, a recipe
for *cordon bleu*. How do you explain these things
to the press, friends and family, the lover
who brushes your cheek with his gifted hands?

III. Queen of Earthquakes

I even watch your disaster movies: *Earthquake, City on Fire.*
    Secretly, I want the ground to open its train-
wrecking embrace, cars to ricochet against high-rises,
    Charlton Heston to leave you for his sunny mistress.
Yes, I want you to die, Ava, in a Pana-vision of doomsday
    Los Angeles: ripped freeways, shattered glass,
a bridge consuming itself in spasms of stupid pleasure.
    The camera never stops shaking. Where is your face?
Let us rewind this holocaust and pause the apocalypse.
    For nature, unlike history, never fails to remind men
of their errors. In Hollywood, the Richter scale repairs
    misdirected passion, realigns the heart's tortured
landscape. Moreover, during an earthquake, no man
    can leave his woman's side. But here you are
drinking in a flamenco club. Here you are breaking
    George C. Scotts's face with a bottle of cheap
Spanish gin. Here you are dying in a hospital in Rome.
    Sinatra's bodyguard nudges you with the Bible;
he mumbles from the Book of Revelations.
    Each word is a sexless cadaver hanging itself.
Indeed, these, your final movies, disaster flicks, are parables

of glamorous discontent. Confess: you want the world
to collapse upon itself, the lovers to be thrown
   into the blaze. Go on, then, Contessa, dance your way
out of this mess. Here's a time machine: Grabtown,
   North Carolina, 1934: you're fresh-faced again, and
nimble. Your bare feet scamper through tobacco fields
   at twilight. And when the terrain shifts, Ava, as the
earth erupts, someone is holding you, once again, too close.

An Usher's Reprimand

The usher must approach two elderly customers who are
unknowingly distracting the audience by talking back to the
screen.
— from *Sample Role Plays*, AMC Theatres Staff Handbook

Ladies, please, as members of the WWII generation,
you both must recognize how much today's noisy,

ill-mannered ticket buyers have cheapened
the special magic of going to the movies. Last year,

in over fifteen privately funded focus groups
conducted around the country, AMC, my employer,

the people who pay my wage, listened to hundreds
of moviegoers express their frustrations with crying

babies, cigarette smoke and sticky floors. Now,
because grumpy and dissatisfied customers are not

what AMC hoped to find, I'm here to tell you
that fellow patrons talking back to the screen

is another common complaint. Myself, I have
an *abuela* who watches Mexican soap operas all day

long, and never, not once, has she counseled,
deprecated, consoled, or felicitated the beautiful

young maid who, having grown up an orphan,
unknowingly works for her lost father,

a handsome millionaire, whose house she cleans,
whose son, her half-brother, she unknowingly and

half-incestuously loves. The father, of course,
has recently discovered his paternity, but,

since his daughter's mother was a prostitute, albeit
a gold-hearted one, he figures the shame

of the revelation would harm the girl somehow.
Also, his efforts to undermine his children's

relationship seem, at least to the children, capricious
if not cruel. You can imagine the complications,

the pins and needles of such a predicament.
But does my *abuela*, alone in her house save for

her deaf and blind husband, talk back to the screen?
No. Instead, she waits for me to arrive home

from work, and then and only then, after preparing me
Cuban coffee with sugar cookies, and maybe some

chocolates, does she share insights and concerns.
It's true that I'm unable to spend time with her

each day, what with my additional burden
of interacting with peers with whom I share

a similar resigned and cynical outlook on life.
Fortunately, she has her crossword puzzles

to occupy her, to keep her silent and contemplative
after the soaps sign off. In sum, ladies, you have

no excuse. While my *abuela*, sofa-bound and noiseless,
a messy, between-commercials game of solitaire

next to her, anticipates the maid to explore
photo albums, here you are, sucking mints

and sipping sodas and admonishing Paul Newman
to comb his hair and mend his jeans. "She's nothing

but a hussy," you caution aloud, even though
it's nothing but celluloid you're speaking to,

and anyway poor Paul's nearly seventy and remains
happily married to Joanne Woodward, and are we

not all hussies to some extent? Naturally, I want you
to enjoy the movie, but I kindly ask that you refrain

from any excessive talking during the movie. Hopefully,
this reprimand will discourage you from talking back

to the screen and unknowingly distracting your fellow
ticket-buying moviegoers. Now, would you be so kind

as to pass me a mint? I love these things
with the chocolate. Thank you.

Godzilla's Waltz
with apologies to Theodore Roethke

The fire on your breath
Made our big city ignite;
But we watched on like gnats:
Such waltzing we could not fight.

You romped until the trains
Slid from the subway tracks;
The scrapers' windowpanes
Hit the ground with a *Crack*!

The foot that crushed those tanks
Was like a bolt of thunder;
At each step you planted,
The troops were torn asunder.

You beat time on our streets
With a fission-powered tail,
Then waltzed back to the sea
Still giddy from the affair.

A Love Story

"WWII pilots took to copying the Varga Girls on the noses of their planes and on various other pieces of military equipment." —from Tom Robotham's Varga

Air Force Boy meets Varga Girl, March '43.
He opens his lucky pocketknife, cuts her free
from *Esquire*, folds her, tucks her safely away

in the handmade chamois-skin pouch
his mother gave him at the station. He's a bomber
pilot from Georgia. She's a bombshell from the airbrush

of a Peruvian artist. It can only end
in disaster; he knows this, doesn't care.
Doesn't care that she's mass-produced,

her eggshell-smooth skin and flawless limbs
decorating the barracks of thousands of GIs.
Doesn't care that the Post Office judges her

obscene. That back home he'd have to keep her
a secret from the freckled sweetheart he'll marry
after the war. None of it matters, because he sees

something in this Varga Girl others can't, something
in the way she looks at him. But his tour is nearly done, so
tonight, lying in his canvas bag, he makes plans to let her go.

Maybe he'll copy her to the 1,000-pound bomb
that hangs from the rack of his twin-engine. Maybe not.
A storm swats the tent with rain, making it hard to sleep.

He takes her out, grabs a flashlight, studies her dreamy gaze,
her cleavage, buttocks. He pictures the two of them together,
soaring high above the black sands of Guadalcanal. He

imagines the Japanese soldier's expression, the thoughts running through the poor bastard's mind, as she drops from the sky, smiling, sinuous. *Angel of light without mercy.*

Interior Monologue for My Plane Crash

Does metal bleed?
I don't think so, darling.

Not fair.

All flight long the stewardess played nurse.
She fixed me up. So that when we started
our descent everything felt
like the swipe
of a cool, moist cotton ball
just before the needle.

black box inside my head black box inside
my head

The engines cut out my heart.
Did they reconstruct yours?
They weren't loud enough, were they?
I thought as much, but there was nothing
I could say. Besides, everyone had on their masks.
Everyone was saddened by the arbitrary practices
of gravity.

Sucking the sucky movie out of our lives?
All the movies we'll never get the chance to watch?
Captain says, *Please check the number and dial again and*
again and
These gruesome snacks, let the angels use them
as confetti.
No, fuck the angels.

There's a party going on right here.
Flying metal is throwing a bash in our honor.
Eviscerating itself for our benefit.

Dearest Jennifer,
I'm going to Long Beach, California,
and you'll have a lot of responsibilities
while I'm gone.

TWO

Upon Visiting the New Orleans Pharmacy Museum
for Liz

How did this place save anyone:
lead-lined baby bottles, creosote
inhalers, needles as long as your
forearm. If these instruments failed
to cure, bring on the leeches.

If leeches failed, behold the barber's
razor. Then, as now, narcotics posed
as medicine: pile salve, anti-bilious
worm powder, heroin for the common
toothache. So why the soda fountain?

Who could stand such drowsy bitters
after a cocaine-powered Coke float?
Though at times cruelly incompetent,
bayou-variety Victorians were also
ingeniously humane. Consider the cleft-

palate pacifier. Or the cyclopean monocle.
Indeed, this museum is a monument
to a warped past, when the pharmacist
made your make-up. When, in New Orleans,
he served as your witch-doctor. Here,

for instance, is a gnarled root on a dish.
A card reads: "John the Conqueror, 25 cents,
novelty." Above sits a push-pin doll.
Her skirt is a red handkerchief fringed
with lace. Her smile is thin, wary.

The Conversion of Aubrey Beardsley

He lies in a white bed, tubercular lungs
hemorrhaging, flecking the white sheets,
the white paper, his pajamas. The dandy
brought down, betrayed. Nature's
imperfect flower, wilting since birth,
always shunning the sun. Now windows
are sealed, the day's dumb spears blocked
by black tapestries. Altar candles suffuse
the room with soft, artificial flickerings,
the method of the symbolists, his hero,
Gustave Moreau. Hair the color of tortoise
shell, face as white as the gardenia on his
lapel, he carefully sits up, strains to prop
the board against his lap, squirts ink on
the page, then draws out from there,
broadening with a brush, correcting lines
with zinc, scraping with a penknife. Dead
at twenty-five, it seems, and he finds that
mortality has diminished his priesthood
in the service of Art. God is on his mind.
The narrow path between atheism and
belief shrinks. But which style to choose?
Intellectual Catholicism? Fine. They'd ask
his confession and have his publisher burn
his pictures, nothing more. Once, as a child,
he saw the bloody crucifix fall from his
bedroom wall. What Wilde would've said
to that! "Morality is always the last refuge
of people who cannot understand beauty."
Dream and reality, each provides its own
pain. Only one can be cheated, so he sketches
the comedians. They gather around the dying
boy, a crowd of costumed clowns, fingers
to their lips, hushing the viewers' laughter,
impertinent remarks, coughing of the damned.

Notes on Lombroso's Theories of Degeneracy

The skull is an aristocrat,
A bone that wants out.
Sockets grow weary
Of their helpless tenants,

Of housing miserable tears,
Of hoarding greasy evil,
Of deferring to the reptilian heart.
Dear jaws, why must you suffer

The rolling pin blows
Of welterweight wives?
Poor cranium, guileless braincase,
What are the slim rewards

For enveloping a mass of putty,
This destitute calculator?
Only the medulla thanks you
For evading the hatchet.

Emergency
for Sean

Hear those sirens? They scavenge
The Playgrounds of Darkness.
Ambulances ferry them from
Body to body, from hospitals

To the places where people
Fuck up: the surreal crash scenes,
The parking lot executions,
The domestic hammer blows.

Sirens are the final warning:
Someone has been rendered
Pale, ghost-like. Someone might
Never wake again. When the alarm

Sounds, prepare for a collision
With terror, a sideswipe at mystery.
There might even be blood, since
The rain washes everything

And nothing. Sirens emit
Deranged intervals, hideous
Scales only God won't hear.
Pain's infinite noise made finite.

Sirens start softly, imperceptibly,
Like the flutter of wings. Gradually,
they grow in momentum, intensity:
A vulture's mad shriek.

Gifted Students

drown. What happens is this: As a child, you
never learn to swim. As a teen, you learn to
smoke crooked joints with conviction, to flick
a switchblade like a frisbee, to slap your mother's
face, to break and enter your ex-girlfriend's
loveless house, to develop a skin-of-your-teeth
liaison with local law enforcement. And you
learn to lie. I forgive you, Jerry, despite your
Judas Priest record collection, your thrash-metal
haircut, and your name, a sinister parallel-universe
version of my own. Your name is the dark mirror,
the hook that drags me into the spotlight.
I forgive you your family. Remember your father?
He held a fifth-degree black belt. He let us throw
knives at the garage door. He left you for Montana.
I hear he fractures the collarbones of drunk Indians.
Remember the afternoon he fixed us sandwiches?
As he clattered the silverware, he asked me
if I wanted white or wheat. Since then, I cannot
recall the last time a man served me a sandwich.
Remember when you divulged your I.Q. score?
It's 142: 43 points lower than Einstein's; 25 points
higher than Ted Bundy's. I never shared mine,
so, yes, you must have rubbed those numbers
into my face, like the bitter paste we used to make
our magazine-shredded collages in our gifted classes.
As gifted students, we dissected a shark, a frog,
two crayfish. With premeditation, we dripped
viscera on the fat kids. At our gifted camps,
we snapped bras, pissed into test tubes,
fed the constrictor the hamster. Later, of course,
I left you for private school where I was birched
for poor penmanship. Meanwhile, you grew up
in an alley near I-275. Most people wouldn't raise
a dog in that neighborhood, so your mother
raised three children. My own mother called

recently to tell me you have drowned.
(Gifted programs don't offer swimming lessons.)
Your friends were too drunk to save you.
In my poem, friends are worthless. In my poem,
our giftedness is worthless. For my tenth birthday,
my father drove us to Adventure Island, the water park
that was built on a landfill. You followed me down
the slide, but you forgot to tell me you couldn't swim.
We hit the pool together, and you splashed around,
flailing and gasping. You were desperate to live,
or to simply breathe. Did I turn to help you, Jerry?
Did I reach out and give you my hand?

for Jerry Baker (1973-1995)

Heart, You're a Hospital Now

Nothing is worse than a dying patient,
Except the surgeon, who gives your life lease,
Cuts you open, removes a sick piece,
Stitches you up, and grows impatient
Of your bloated face. No wonder he dons
A mask, gloves. His scalpel is a scepter.
He's a priest to whom God must pray. Better
To chew prescriptions than become pain's pawn.

Darkness congeals like a forgotten bruise.
Tonight you will salvage narcotic bliss.
Each tablet, capsule, injection and dose
Is an angel kissing you with scarred lips.
Nurses read your chart over and again.
Nothing? No more pain? Then close the curtain.

So Loved the World

Take away her leg.
Take away one breast,

then the other.
Take away her hair, Lord.

Take away her strength with cancer-fighting
drugs, with the burning light

of radiation. *Your heavenly finger?*
Take away her mind, Lord. It grows

dimmer in the chasm of mortality,
in the darkness of last days.

So take it away. Take away her access
to halfway-decent care. Make her carefree.

Fill her lungs with fluid. *Drain them fill*
them drain them fill them again O Lord again

Give her a clean white room.
With a window, please. A view of the sky

and the parking lot. Give her bedside flowers.
Give her a nice painless death. Lord,

give her that much.

Black Revolver

Cock-
ed and forever loaded. Bonecrusher, meatgrinder, brain-
splatterer.
Weapon of individual destruction. Hitler's rock-hard
brush.
Widow maker spreads
Everywhere: ghetto, schoolyard,
Workplace. Dead
Flowers hang from
Its snout. Whore of
Metal, powder, pin.

Litany for the Faithless

The sound of prepuberty
Hints to all things heavenly:
Angel, cloud, white rosary.
Listen to the choirboy sing

Sotto voce, undertone,
Like a child who prays alone,
An orphan dialing God's phone.
Listen to the choirboy sing

Forte, young David's slingshot,
Scourge of Old Testament thought:
We murder what loves Him not.
Listen to the choirboy sing

Tunes composed to combat sin:
Mary's sleep-inducing hymn;
Jesus' big, black requiem.
Listen to the choirboy sing.

Writing Against God

Requires infinite patience. Angelic repose.
Quiet. A room of glassy-eyed demons
In a highway motel no one else knows.

Something to write with. Black feather.
Inkwell of warm blood. Paper? Pages ripped
From the Gideon. No deadlines, either.

The stakes are enormous. So just write long.
The outline alone can snuff your best years.
In the next room, your poor wine-drunk Mom.

Funeral Speaker

Even as the furnace burns,
Choking the sky with smoke,
You go on and on
Like a late-night monster movie.

Every word a ruined metropolis.

Orator of the damned,
Goat-faced auctioneer,
Perched atop a battered stool,
Pinching the fleshy waitresses,
Daring the world's most depraved fry cook
To eighty-six your chili dog.
How long must you continue to sell
Highly personal interpretations
Of someone's laminated menu?

And who can eat with you mouthing off?
Must be the stale pepper making us sneeze.
Also, the forks are dirty, the napkins stained.
The counter might double as an Altar of Sin.

Place your final offering there.

Lunch Hour Facelift

I'd brought a sandwich, just in case.
In the waiting room sat the detectives,
Their punitive eyes intent
On the clock's illicit second hand.

Greasy magazines for everyone to touch.
The music was pure Sunday-school terror,
Noises like those a doomed submarine makes
On its way to the ocean floor.

My ears will pop, someone blurted out.
A new breed of slasher film, remarked another.
Reaching into my coat for a tissue,
I found instead an expired pet store coupon.
No one conceded the mud-caked carpet.

There was also a painting, I remember.
A man dying at a table,
A bone lodged in his throat.
I could almost hear him coughing.
Or was it the doctor's assistant?

Here she comes now, the Lurid Plaything.
She peeks from behind the door,
An all-too familiar name
On the tip of her bloodless tongue.

Scoped

"The pain stayed until I knew its childlike
Cruelty and innocence,
Its pettiness too."
— Charles Simic

I'd been passing blood, so I go
to the urologist. There I am in a
so-clean-it-smells examination
room with my pants down and
some guy is flipping my testicles
around like supermarket lemons,
asking me what hurts. "Nothing,"
I say. He tells me to turn over on
my side and pull my knees against
my chest. The glove snaps. And
sure enough, he's got his finger
inside of me, poking around.
"Does this hurt?" "No," I say,
"but it doesn't feel good either."
Afterwards, more tests, probes,
injections. The lady doctor is very
patient and understanding as she
pumps radioactive iodine into my
veins. Days later, I carry the X-
rays to the urologist who studies
them, decides that more tests are
needed. He says I must be scoped,
thoroughly scoped. And so I'm
back in the so-clean-it-smells room,
seated in a special chair. The doctor
enters with a cart full of tools, his
dungeon-torture kit, picks up this
THING about a foot-and-a-half
long, the diameter of a ball-point
pen, and says he's going to insert it
into my penis. And after shoving that

THING all the way to my bladder, it
turns out that all along I've had an
inflamed prostate. But now I have an
inflamed prostate into which someone
has inserted a THING. "Blood in the
urine for the next week," the doctor
assures me, "will be entirely normal."
Twenty patients later, the doctor goes
home and says to his wife, "Honey,
I looked at this guy's prostate today,
and guess what? He's a poet—can you imagine?"

Ventriloquism Made Easy

He called me Sawdust Brains.
Doll-dummy. Mr. Trick Talker.
I searched for comebacks,
But words were pebbles
Clattering impotently
In the hollow of my hinged mouth.

Spineless, save for his clumsy mitt,
I sat there, a monocled slave,
Chained to the oars of the audience's laughter.
I wore comedy the way a priest dons
His vestment, dutifully, as if at any moment
The stars might go out.
During one performance, they did,
But even in darkness, I could sense

The spectators' lips silently moving.

The Love Song of Alfred E. Neuman

"After Mad, *drugs were nothing."* — Patti Smith

Let us worry then, you and I,
When the fold-in reveals itself as a high
Like Clint Eastwood cowpunched in a stable;
Let us worry about blow-your-mind drug primers,
Idiot-proof typewriters
Divorce survival merit badges
And endless, futile, Spy vs. Spy gadgets;
Spoofs that prove the criminality
Of Letterman's lack of originality
To bring you once again to my gap-toothed grin....
Oh, do not ask for the Viagra edition!
Let us worry and renew our subscriptions.

In the magazine racks readers can be seen
Mouthing the word
Potrzebie!

Hair

I was a teenage Samson
On a planet of Delilahs,
All threatening to shear me.
My mother. A math teacher.
A cousin who claimed I resembled
A notorious Islamic terrorist.
And Dad? He simply shook
His paramilitary head.

One day after raking and mowing
My parents' yard, I relaxed
In the patio with a comic book.
My sister walked over, saw a lizard
Perched in my hair, and screamed.

Afterwards, I got a crewcut.

I recall Dad driving me to the barber's.
In an upholstered chair, I braced
For scissors, electric razor, the blade.
I prepared for something to leap
From its cozy thicket, out into a world
Of noise and brutal light. I wanted to be
The first to say, *Little one, do not worry.*
Though your home is gone, there's always
A place for you in my shirt pocket.
Or this—here is my open hand.

Mother Delilah

In a town called Black Massacre, it's her
All the curly-headed galoots desire. She keeps
A gas-lit room in the No Chance Saloon.
If she's not there, try the gambling machines.

Whiskey-drenched, she'll belt murder ballads
To amuse the card players, with their braying
And bad hygiene. But she's always ready to give
A swift, brutal cut: first, she takes your six-gun,

Then, *snip snip*. Don't fret the scissors;
They're stainless. The silver mirror
She hides under her velvet pillow is for
The smallest boy. He never sheds a tear.

Punk Rockers

"And when they all were seated,
A service like a drum
Kept beating, beating, till I thought
My mind was numb."
— Emily Dickinson

Tonight everyone plays the outlaw.
Tonight everyone gets his phone call.
Pre-shaved, branded and marked,
Already herded in the chamber's dark,

Puppets hook themselves to their strings.
Bring on the Noise of the Machine.
Satan's own choirboy vomits his score,
Splatters the sludge of the killing floor.

Drums cannon the fodder's brains.
Bass blasts a dummy's chest with pain.
Guitar slashes the victims' ears;
Lambs twitching under razored shears.

Generation KKK, no one gets away,
No matter if these bloodstains fade.
Don't want to heed the protest song?
Won't hurt to play it all night long.

Lab Animal Newsletter

Everyone wants to ride ride ride
Our humane animal treadmill:

Interning students. Cleaning staff.
Even the white-coated scientists are itching

For a taste of electrical stimulus.
They grow tired of the computer screen's

Cynical glow; they want a jolt of faith.
How about our volumetric drinking monitor?

In the past, animal hydration was measured
By counting animal licks on the dispenser.

Today our product employs a novel principle
Based on the precise measurement

Of licks licks licks. How about a water maze?
The tracking of animals can be automated

By using a video system. The maze itself
Is constructed of stainless steel, which has been painted

Black. Everything listed contains a current far below
The threshold of an animal's sensitivity.

Cut-Rate Liquor

I

The sign says NO CHECKS!
There's no one to guide you.
Ask for the product by its name.
Don't touch anything but your wallet.

Everything in this store is heavy.
Vodka squats in oversized jugs.
The beaujolais runs darker than blood.
Here even champagne is gravity's slave.

In the adjacent lounge, drinks are named
After poisonous snakes. Cigarette smoke
Drifts across a gallery of ruined faces. Hours later,
The whiskey tastes like iced tea.

Blinds you.

The ditch digger crumples ones and fives.
The labor pooler jangles pocket change.
The toothless solicitor kneels,
Cups his drool in his hands.

The homeless always pay more.

Back outside, someone will confront you,
Some rotten, wing-clipped angel in third-hand rags.
Give him a dollar, but don't touch his filthy hands.
Look at his face, but don't let him speak.
Silence him with tales of baby Jesus.
Ask innocently if he accepts his own heart.

Lie and make him promise to steal.

2

This angel will mouth an incantation:
I was once a high school football star.
I was a helicopter pilot in Nam.
I play the harmonica, no, the bag pipes,
Your sister's trombone. I was injured by a tractor.
My wife shot me three times in the back.
Jesus put me here to read the funnies.
Over 300 white women have consented to enjoy
Sexual experiences with me. In the summer,
I punch horses. As you can plainly see,
I'm half machine, half polar bear.
This is why my ass never freezes in Antarctica.

In your hand, the dollar hangs.
A strip of skin.

So follow his haunted stride
As the sun mocks the moon.
He leads you past dog shit,
Through a bottle-littered parking lot,
Under a devil's streetlight.
He opens the door for you.
Enter a miserable dimension where
Everything is for sale and
Everything is an endless cure.
Ask for the product by its name.
Gather your crumbled bills.
The line for the broken

Starts here.

Questions I've Yet To Ask My Father, a Fireman

Do you repress the primal urge,
as Freud suggests, to extinguish
a fire by urination? Has a stranger
ever asked you for a match?

The human heart: tender or tinder?
Why do torch songs radiate blue
light? If the world burns, will the meek
inherit ash? If the world burns

with desire, who are the meek?
Do you dream of conflagrations?
Say you're to be smothered:
Would you prefer drowning in iced

water or superheated smoke? Can you
recall the patron saint of firemen?
Whom has he ever helped? Did you
know Abraham built a fire altar where

he planned to sacrifice his only son?

Captain America at Home
for Jack Kirby

After a long day of cracking Red Skull's
skull, he is sofa-bound, polishing the star-
spangled shield that protects him from
the transforming powers of the Cosmic
Cube, the swarming gadgetry of Baron
Zemo, the deadly karate chops of the
Super-Adaptoids. For now, he is happy.
The TV is on, background noise he needs
to drown his fears and concentrate;
the gauntlets, literally, are off. Tonight
he will shine his shield, stitch his winged
mask, and catch a few sound bites on
Headline News. That's the plan.

But then the unthinkable occurs: he sees
that the white star of his jersey contains
a bloodstain in the shape of his country's
mainland, forty-eight states, all of which
he's saved more than once from mind-
control, mass murder, General Mayhem.
He ponders the magnitude of his job,
the awesome responsibility of defending
not only the land of freedom but also the
free world. It seems too much, really,
for one man alone. Which is how he feels
most of the time, isolated from the citizenry
he has sworn to protect. For a moment,

he ponders life without a country,
a nomadic existence, a self-imposed exile,
allowing his lungs to swell proudly,
like birthday balloons. To inhale *clean* air,
air minus the taint of patriotism, Puritanism,
"mobocracy." To talk with people as if
they were real, not just some glorified

abstraction. *But enough!* He shakes himself
like a wet dog, gets up to toss the soiled
jersey into the washer. Meanwhile, the bald
eagle statuette that squats atop his mantelpiece
squints fiercely and prepares for flight.

Road Runner Blues

*"Solitude is fine, but you need someone to tell you that
solitude is fine."* — Balzac

A bird that runs. Flying fish
    Of the land. Funny by the way
It moves, not what it looks like.
    Plunks its tongue. Velocity
Makes the blacktop ribbon up
    From the ground. (*Accelleratii
Incredibus.*) Wile E. will fail.
    What is unknown is its apparatus—
How the coyote will fail. Zoom and
    Bored. Immune to ACME-brand
Earthquake Pills. *Meep meep*s its way
    Out of any bind. Carefree,
Uncatchable, and always on the run.
    A moving target. Smiling symbol
Of everyone's miserable toil,
    Of the world's frustrated dream.

Coyote Blues

"A fanatic is someone who redoubles his effort when he has forgotten his aim." — George Santayana

ACME, Wile E.? It's just nutsy
Gadgetry, ingenious but terrifically
Flawed: Do-It-Yourself Tornadoes,
Axle Grease (Guaranteed Slippery),
And Rocket Powered Roller Skates
Are variations on a theme of self-
Destruction. *Carnivorous vulgaris*,
You're a Hopalong Casualty, a real
Sisyphus-figure pushing Dehydrated
Boulders up the hill. When it rains—
Lickety splat—you're literally flattened.
No road runner burger for you,
So try again and again *ad infinitum*.
Comedy as repetition-compulsion?
Chase parody as paradigm? Does your
Failure hurt less if we interpret it? Hey,
I know it's hard to get things done:
Someone's always *meep meep*-ing at
The crucial moment, and life becomes
A spot-gag for other people's pleasure.
Soon we find we're no longer at war
With the bird, but with ourselves.
Stuck in a sunny, sultry desert, we hunger
For a scrap of zestily-drawn dignity.

Comic Book Saint

In a Catholic bookstore, you find
the four-color story of a woman
who cured the sightless and repelled

heathen soldiers. It is lodged among
plastic rosaries and various artificial
Jesuses. Now God is a comic book

by which we measure the pain of others,
particularly the saints. Open it,
and everything stands revealed,

like the mechanism of an ancient weapon,
smug in its crudity. *Page 1 / panel 1*:
Claire consecrates herself by cutting her hair.

Her speech balloon is inflated with pieties,
sacred oaths, divine love. Yet, already,
it sags with the weight of martyrdom,

holiest of death wishes. *Page 3 / panel 5*:
caption bleeds into blessed background:
Francis's new, improved Eden (cutting edge

of petting zoos) provides sanctuary
for Christians with their vows of silence,
poverty, chastity, all the promises

that deny an animal her animal side.
No wrenching sound effects here. Only
the introspective puff of bubbles of deep

thought. *Page 11 / panel 13*: Claire strikes
down her father's hand. He will never
forgive her; he hates Claire's presumption

as much as the Pope scorns her habit
of poor sisters. Page seven is full
of the death of Saint Claire. God works

His mysterious illness, rendering her pale,
ghost-like. Is this the price one pays
for devoting oneself to omnipotence?

Where are the ads for blackhead removers?
Confess! You gave pieces of silver in exchange
for this curiosity. Double-bag, please,

because you have faith
that in fifty years the material value
will have amassed. *Pow!*

THREE

After Reading "Harold's Purple Crayon"

The sun. The moon. Draw
the stars. A road so long you can walk
many miles. A vast ocean without monsters.
A trim little sailboat. A beach

upon which to rest and enjoy nine kinds
of purple pies. A hungry moose
to finish the crusts. A mountain
to climb. A balloon to carry you

through clouds. A rocket that fires
you into orbit and beyond. A parachute
for your return. A policeman who raises
his baton, points the way to another page

in which you draw the girl
you will marry, and the child you will raise,
who renders the stars, moon, and sun,
just as you have done right here, like so.

Wedding Bells

Sure, I was an usher, but nobody told me
beforehand to seat mothers and their new
husbands in the front. Marriage time,
my mother-in-law approaches, pissed off
that her ex-husband is seated closer to the altar
than her. "It's traditional," she insists,
"for the mother to sit there." How curious,
I think, for the divorced to invoke nuptial
tradition. But she's my mother-in-law,
and I want to make her happy, so I walk
down the aisle solo (the other ushers
probably sense trouble), and I tell my father-in-law,
"Mr. Bigshot Priest says mothers in the first row,
fathers in the second." "No problem," he says,
and I return to bask in the light of my mother-in-law's
praise. "Go back," says the bride's mother,
who's no relation to me, at least not just yet, but still
an intimidating woman in her own right.
"Tell my ex to sit in the second row, too."
"OK, OK," I say, and I'm feeling fortunate
that her ex is nowhere to be seen, probably
somewhere writing a check, so I get his new wife
to move, easy as pie, and I'm walking back with a huge
smile, a defender of tradition, when he grabs my elbow.
"Why did you move my wife?" His nostrils flare,
his lips compress, and for a moment I believe
he is going to start yelling, but then organ music
fills the church, bells clang, and as I'm gesturing
that the noise is too much, can't hear, his grip tightens,
and in steps the bride, my wife a bridesmatron. They look
delighted to see us guys together, arm in arm, collecting
ourselves, almost ready to see another perfect couple off
into a world of love and trust and faithfulness.

The Yoganaut
for Jennifer

I sometimes refer to my wife
in the presence of others as "the yoganaut."
Though lately my skepticism towards her
routine has weakened. During her stretches
and postures, she seems so content,
so relaxed, that I begin to suffer
pangs of envy. When she performs
Sun Salutations, a beatific smile grips
her face. This, of course, causes me
to examine my own smile,
which appears sad in comparison.
She is capable of many feats:
she can do push-ups upside down,
stand on her head, and bend her body
into a bow. Once, I checked out
a library book about all the different kinds
of "yogic" poses, and when I related them
to my wife she laughed at their names:
Scalp Yanking, Alternate Nostril Breathing,
Cobra Locust Bend. However, she was
in fact familiar with Lion Pose, of which
she gave a demonstration by sitting on
her heels, leaning forward, and sticking out
her tongue as the hot damp of the jungle
rose in the room and the lesser animals
cried out in terror, in desire.

Crowded Rooms

"If I'm in someplace crowded, I need to be, like,
over against a wall." — some guy in a coffeehouse

We are not men, but agoraphobes.
We arrange ourselves like sentries
around the perimeters of crowded
rooms, near the fringes of rock concerts
and bar-mitzvahs, on the outskirts of wine
tastings and wet T-shirt contests. Silently,
we dust the potted plants, admire the baby grand,
stoically guard the crackers and seafood
dip.

We are extra furniture,
greasy diner gunfighters,
nightclub speed bumps,
high school reunion gargoyles,
robots to bring in the new year.

Outside, we decorate your cookouts.

We would unite, but we're a little edgy.

Meantime, our shoulderblades tease
freshly painted walls of new houses.
Our shoes leave imprints in the muted
rugs of art galleries.
Our hands crumple the same frail napkin.

Our eyes?
Everywhere.

Our National Anthem

It's New Year's Eve, and I'm drinking
with straight friends in a gay sports bar.
Charlie the bartender serves us sequined
tiaras, party horns, leis, and bottles of Bud.
"Oops," says Trish, "I just got laid."

Nobody responds, because our eyes
are glued to the giant screen, where sumo
wrestlers are repeatedly walloping each other.
"Diapers," snorts Doug. Fortunately,
Nathan, a PhD candidate, has been to Japan

and speaks with authority. "Not diapers,"
he says. "*Mawashis*. And they're made
of the finest silk." Then, before one
of us can ask him if he's ever tried on a mawashi,
a transvestite kickstarts tonight's karaoke

with an eardrum-busting rendition of Prince's
"When Doves Cry." Trish swigs her beer
and sings along. Or is she just lip-synching?
Doug palms some pretzels. I ask Nathan,
"Hey, Nathan. Why do they grab each other's

mawashis?" He says, "To unbalance
the opponent. Isn't it obvious?" I say,
"I don't know. Maybe they like the sensation."
Doug signals Charlie for another round, and I'm starting
to feel unbalanced myself. The falsetto crooning.

The foreign wrestling. The domestic beer.
I'm thinking there's got to be a better way to greet
the new century than in a half-empty gay sports bar
in downtown Columbus, Ohio. Reading my mind,
Doug says, "Why are we here? We're not gay

and we hate sports," and Trish replies, "It's snowing,
and this was the closest place." Now a different
transvestite takes the stage and launches into "Grease."
"This song makes me think of the late Roman empire,"
says Nathan. And I'm thinking this is the craziest

thing I've ever heard. That is, until Doug says, "Ahh.
Our national anthem." Suddenly everything clicks,
and I realize that all along I was fated to cross
the millennial threshold in this bar, with these friends,
and drink this brand of American beer, and sing

this tune of independence that goes, *Grease is the word,*
is the word that you heard, it's got groove, it's got
meaning, and watch helplessly as Trish asks Nate
why sumo don't grease their bods beforehand,
and what else can one say to that but *Hail, Glorious Caesar?*

Graduate Student Gets Drunk After Reading Critical Terms for Literary Study

Liquor makes everything easy.
For example, my heart feels,
at this precise moment, like it could savagely
beat the world's cons right back
into their texts. Also, my brain
is now a cruel weapon of psychoanalytic
defenestration. I could strip
this lounge and its inhabitants down
to core hysterias and gynocidal
assumptions. I was trained to do this,
I'm a graduate student. No one is safe.
Lock up your dodge-drafters! Otherwise,
take a number, because this cut-rate
martini renders me increasingly invincible.
The sulfites alone fortify with enough
essential vitamins and minerals to kill
a family of four for three months.
Two days ago, I was one sorry surgeon
general. Tonight not even a machine
can impair my ability to operate
a birth defect. So what if I'm pregnant?
My health problems are not mine
and nobody else's. I'm a Challenger
of the Unknown, one of four rugged
adventurers who miraculously survived
a plane crash. "We're living on borrowed
time," said the bald one. Or maybe we
spoke those words simultaneously.
Regardless, we endured true menace
from strange threats: The sorcerous
descendant of Merlin, an outer space child
who wanted to keep us as pets, a futuristic
Gestapo. We defeated them all.
Now here we are in this flashy establishment,
juking the boxes, screwing the drivers.

Nothing could be better. Except for this
drink. Hegemony Cricket, it needs work,
though, at least on the surface of things,
it appears to be working just fine.

Hangover Remedy

"Greasy bacon and mayo sandwich," said my good friend,
    Byron, not the legendary poet of course, but the country
And western disc jockey who doesn't jockey any discs,
    But instead pushes buttons on a computer, triggering
Big patches of songs with titles like "Whose Bed
    Have Your Boots Been Under," and at times switches
On the mike to announce upcoming events

Like the "2000 Monster Truck Rally in Tallahassee!"
    And is always writing poems in the control booth
With titles like "Raccoons: A Vision in Three Parts,"
    And is always winning contests with these poems,
And I'm talking *real* contests, the kind that pay money—
    Fifty bucks here, a hundred there—while I write more
Serious stuff, with titles like "Writing Against God,"

Some of which gets published in obscure literary mags
    That pay zip, and I spend weeks—sometimes months—
On these things, and it burns me up that Byron can just sit
    Down in a sterile booth in some corporate office park
And write against the bad music that's booming in his ears
    And clock out with a brand new poem that's fated to win
An award. I mean, getting paid to write poems! And me?

Do I get paid to write? No, I make money by grading
    Hundreds of freshmen papers on the pros and cons
Of binge drinking, and when the tediousness of it all
    Crushes my spirit, I walk to the corner bar and drink
And think about how I'll never have a job that allows me
    To write poems, much less poems of any financial
Merit, and after a few pricey martinis I stumble home,

Go to bed, wake up with a hangover, a pounding
    In my brain. I break out the frying pan and the slimy
Bacon and the mayo and I toast the bread, and there
    I am in my kitchen, staring at an ugly lump of grease,

Hoping it will kill the pain I've inflicted on myself
And give me the necessary strength to sit down
At my desk and write until the throbbing eases,
The words start coming, and O the sweet sun!

A Bright Future for Poets

*"Palestinian leader Yasser Arafat gave a pistol to a poet
and said to shoot him if he betrayed the Palestinian people."*
— Associated Press newswire, December 6, 1999

The pistol is mightier than the sword.
And in a poet's hand, the pistol is God's
thunder crack, disintegrating a nation's
Judas. Is this what Shelley meant when

he called the poet "the unacknowledged
legislator of all mankind"? Shouldn't all
countries adopt a similar program?
Why wait for probes and hearings to drag

their way to vague, unsatisfying conclusions?
Instead, let a poet play judge. Who better
to right what's wrong than the Spokesperson
of the People? Power to the Poets! Prime

Minister Blair, supply Ted Hughes a hunting
permit and rifle. Mr. Clinton, lend Maya
Angelou a four-shot, pearl-handled derringer.
There are absolutely no firearms allowed

in Scandinavia, so whoever's in charge
can furnish his favorite poet with a bow
and arrow. Let the Benedict Arnold there
beware. Though when he hears a *twang!*

at least he'll be able to duck.

The Poet's Bad Faith

It is a shadow of a shadow, only
more tangible. Like an illness, yet
harder to diagnose. It risks distortion.
For what? Personal expression?
Truth? To know the ideal world's

first radioactive giant-monster?
It is a massive opiate. The poet
designs each word to act as a sleeping pill,
a professor's abstract lecture,
a sermon about lifeless angels

dressed in white so bright. It causes
blindness, unleashes desires
better left leashed, repressed, dreamed.
Pits one against science. Makes one
a cheerleader for natural isolation;

for manic, sorrowful drug experiences;
for out-of-body love affairs;
for the ecstasy of agony. It traffics
in oppressive forms of linguistics.
It is a slave ship of slavers, drifting, delinquent. Still,

everyone climbs on board.

Last Book Before World's End

Stalking the house
  Looking for someone

To read passages to.
  Getting on the phone,

If it comes to that.
  Dog-earing the epilogue.

Drinking red wine.
  Waiting for nightfall.

Lighting a candle before
  Studying the appendices.

Writing a salutary review
  That begins, "A book

For all times and places..."
  Outside, hungry crows

Pecking at the remains
  Of a downed kite. Dawn:

Cotton-ball cloud dabbing
  The sky's slashed wrists.

Highway Poem

"Stop, drop, and roll won't help you in hell."
— church sign on Highway 421 near Sunshine, Kentucky

Nothing helps.

Not the highway of encroaching darkness.
Not the headlights of faith.
Not the angels.

Not the plastic Jesus glued to the dash.
Not the Saint of Smash-ups.
Not the rosary
click-clacking on the rearview.
Not the green air freshener
shaped like a tree.

If a hitchhiker thumbs you,
accelerate.
If the car speeds out of your control,
     hits an embankment, explodes,
     don't bother to drop and roll,
     because nothing helps,
and still the flames grow hotter.

Not the 32-ounce Big Gulp.
Not the beef jerky intended for dogs
     and pro-wrestling fans.
Not the road map to Disney and back.
Not the radio of hillbilly voices
     praying for terror, release.
Not the loveliest star.

Not even the radar gun penetrating
     your inescapable mind.

Acknowledgments

These poems first appeared, often in different versions, in the following magazines, to whose editors a grateful acknowledgment is made: *5AM, ACM, Amelia, American Literary Review, The Amherst Review, The Anthology of New England Writers, Apalachee Review, Art:Mag, Art Times: Commentary & Resource for the Fine & Performing Arts, Atlanta Review, Aura Literary Arts Review, Asheville Poetry Review, The Carolina Quarterly, The Chattahoochee Review, Chelsea, Coal City Review, Cold Mountain Review, The Comstock Review, The Connecticut Review, Dogwood: A Journal of Poetry & Prose, The 2000 Emily Dickinson Award Anthology, The Florida Review, Global City Review, The Green Hills Literary Lantern, Hawaii Review, HazMat Review, Idle Hands, Imperial Luau, Iodine, Kansas English: The Journal of the Kansas Association of Teachers of English, Karamu, Kimera, The Laurel Review, Little Brown Poetry, Louisiana Literature, The Louisiana Review, Lullwater Review, Luna Negra, Maelstrom, Main Street Rag, NEBO: A Literary Journal, New Delta Review, OnTheBus, The Oregon Review, Parnassus Literary Journal, Passages North, Paterson Literary Review, Poems & Plays, Poetry Motel, Pop Poets, Porter Gulch Review, Prairie Winds, River King, River Styx, The Savannah Literary Journal, Shattered Wig, Sheridan Edwards Review, Slant, Smartish Pace, The South Carolina Review, The Sow's Ear Poetry Review, Tar River Poetry, Troubadour, Tulane Review, Visions International, Washington Square,* and *Westview: A Journal of Western Oklahoma.*

About The Cover

Comics artist Ken Steacy inked and digitally painted this piece from an original Jack Kirby pencil drawing. The central figure is related to a character created by Jack Kirby in 1971: Big Barda, who first appeared in *New Gods* Vol. 1 and *Mister Miracle* #4 (DC Comics). A warrior from the planet Apokolips, Big Barda battles to protect the Earth from her mortal enemy, Darkseid.

About The Author

The son of a Tampa firefighter, Jarret Keene was born in 1973. He received his Ph.D. in English from Florida State University, Tallahassee, where he served for a number of years as the editor of *Sundog: The Southeast Review*. As well as being a frequent contributor to the *Las Vegas Mercury*, he also teaches literature and creative writing at the University of Nevada, Las Vegas.

Manic D Press Books

This Too Can Be Yours. Beth Lisick. $13.95
Devil Babe's Big Book of Postcards. Isabel Samaras. $11.95
Harmless Medicine. Justin Chin. $13.95
Depending on the Light. Thea Hillman. $13.95
Escape from Houdini Mountain. Pleasant Gehman. $13.95
Poetry Slam: the competitive art of performance poetry. Gary Glazner, ed. $15
I Married An Earthling. Alvin Orloff. $13.95
Cottonmouth Kisses. Clint Catalyst. $12.95
Fear of A Black Marker. Keith Knight. $11.95
Red Wine Moan. Jeri Cain Rossi. $11.95
Dirty Money and other stories. Ayn Imperato. $11.95
Sorry We're Close. J. Tarin Towers. $11.95
Po Man's Child: a novel. Marci Blackman. $12.95
The Underground Guide to Los Angeles. Pleasant Gehman, ed. $14.95
The Underground Guide to San Francisco. Jennifer Joseph, ed. $14.95
Flashbacks and Premonitions. Jon Longhi. $11.95
The Forgiveness Parade. Jeffrey McDaniel. $11.95
The Sofa Surfing Handbook. Juliette Torrez, ed. $11.95
Abolishing Christianity and other short pieces. Jonathan Swift. $11.95
Growing Up Free In America. Bruce Jackson. $11.95
Devil Babe's Big Book of Fun! Isabel Samaras. $11.95
Dances With Sheep. Keith Knight. $11.95
Monkey Girl. Beth Lisick. $11.95
Bite Hard. Justin Chin. $11.95
Next Stop: Troubletown. Lloyd Dangle. $10.95
The Hashish Man and other stories. Lord Dunsany. $11.95
Forty Ouncer. Kurt Zapata. $11.95
The Unsinkable Bambi Lake. Bambi Lake with Alvin Orloff. $11.95
Hell Soup: the collected writings of Sparrow 13 LaughingWand. $8.95
The Ghastly Ones & Other Fiendish Frolics. Richard Sala. $9.95
King of the Roadkills. Bucky Sinister. $9.95
Alibi School. Jeffrey McDaniel. $11.95
Signs of Life: channel-surfing through '90s culture. Joseph, ed. $12.95
Beyond Definition. Blackman & Healey, eds. $10.95
The Rise and Fall of Third Leg. Jon Longhi. $9.95
Specimen Tank. Buzz Callaway. $10.95
The Verdict Is In. edited by Kathi Georges & Jennifer Joseph. $9.95
The Back of a Spoon. Jack Hirschman. $7
Baroque Outhouse/Decapitated Head of a Dog. Randolph Nae. $7
Graveyard Golf and other stories. Vampyre Mike Kassel. $7.95
Bricks and Anchors. Jon Longhi. $8
Greatest Hits. edited by Jennifer Joseph. $7
Lizards Again. David Jewell. $7
The Future Isn't What It Used To Be. Jennifer Joseph. $7

Please add $4 to all orders for postage and handling.
Manic D Press • Box 410804 • San Francisco CA 94141 USA
info@manicdpress.com   www.manicdpress.com